Kid Pick!

Title: _____

Author: _____

Picked by: _____

_____

Why I love this book:

_____

_____

J 7
Sie
Sch

Children's Catalog

Schoolyard

Selected by
Judy Sierra

Kids' Own Rhymes for Rope Skipping,
Hand Clapping, Ball Bouncing,
and Just Plain Fun

Alfred A. Knopf   New York

Rhymes

Illustrated by

Melissa Sweet

t before. A lemon and a pickle came knocking at my door. I went downstairs to let them, let them in. They hit me on the head with a ro

ling pin. Not last night, but the night before. A lemon and a pickle came knocking at n

head with a rolling pin. Not last night lemon and a pickle came knocking at my door. I went downstairs to let them in. They hit me on the

t last night lemon and a pickle came knocking at my door. I went downstairs to let them in. They hit me on the

Introduction

Schoolyard rhymes are catchy and fun. They are easy to remember. In fact, they stick in the mind like bubble gum to a shoe. They create a perfect beat for rope skipping, hand clapping, ball bouncing, and ring games. Rhyming taunts expose kids who break the schoolyard code of honor.

"Liar, liar, pants on fire, nose as long as a telephone wire."
"Copycat, dirty rat, stole my mother's baseball bat."

Many rhymes are pure nonsense. I remember the joy of learning and reciting, "Ladies and jellybeans, hoboes and tramps, cross-eyed mosquitoes and bow-legged ants, I come before you to stand behind you to tell you something I know nothing about. . . ." Poems like these are often chanted by a whole group of children, followed by torrents of giggles.

Amazingly, in this age of fast-changing entertainment, kids are jumping and playing to many of the same rhymes as their great-grandparents. No one knows how old these rhymes are. They have only been collected and published for around 150 years, and have not changed much during that time. Some have been forsaken, and a few new ones have entered the collective memory. Kids clap and skip to popular songs, then forget them. Meanwhile, the silly adventures of doctors, teachers, policemen, weird boyfriends, and the mythical "Lady with the Alligator Purse" have endured for a hundred years.

Schoolyard rhymes of English-speaking countries are very much alike. The exact words vary from place to place and country to country. Knickers (a British synonym for underpants) are popular in rhymes from outside the United States, for example. Christopher Columbus is a character in rhymes from North America, while Captain Cook stars in ones from Australia and New Zealand.

Each new generation of kids claims these rhymes as its own, but of course even the most serious adults once knew and loved them. The traditional poems of childhood create bonds between generations. Look in this book for rhymes you know and rhymes you don't, for your favorites and your parents' and teachers' favorites. Make up a new line or a new verse for an old rhyme, perform it for your friends, and see if it sticks. You can be a playground poet, too.

—Judy Sierra
July 2005

Policeman! Policeman! Do your duty.
Here comes Miss American Beauty.
She can do the pom-poms,
She can do the twist.
Most of all,
She can do the splits.

Anna Banana
Can play the piano.
All she can play
Is "The Star-Spangled Banner."
Anna
  Banana
      Split.

Miss Mary Mack, Mack, Mack,
All dressed in black, black, black,
With silver buttons, buttons, buttons
All down her back, back, back.
She cannot read, read, read,
She cannot write, write, write,
But she can smoke, smoke, smoke
Her daddy's pipe, pipe, pipe.
She asked her mother, mother, mother
For fifty cents, cents, cents
To see the elephants, elephants, elephants
Jump over the fence, fence, fence.
They jumped so high, high, high,
They touched the sky, sky, sky,
And they never came back, back, back
Till the Fourth of July-ly-ly.

3

Fudge, fudge, tell the judge,
Mama's got a newborn baby.
Wrap it up in tissue paper,
Send it down the elevator.
How many pounds did it weigh?
1 - 2 - 3 - 4 - 5 - 6 - 7

said the lady with the alligator purse. Out went the doctor, out went the nurse. Out went the lady with Tiny Tim in her purse. Miss Susie had a baby. His na

with Tiny Tim in her purse. the doctor called the nurse. The nurse called the lady with the alligator purse. "Mumps!" said the doctor. "Measles!" said the nurse.

bathtub but it wouldn't go down his th

Miss Susie had a baby. His name was Tiny Tim.
She put him in the bathtub to see if he could swim.
He drank up all the water, he ate up all the soap.
He tried to eat the bathtub but it wouldn't go down his throat.
Miss Susie called the doctor, the doctor called the nurse,
The nurse called the lady with the alligator purse.
"Mumps!" said the doctor. "Measles!" said the nurse.
"Nothing," said the lady with the alligator purse.
Out went the doctor, out went the nurse.
Out went the lady with Tiny Tim in her purse.

roat. Miss Susie called

5

Oh, my, my.
I want a piece of pie.
Pie too sweet.
I want a piece of meat.
Meat too tough.
I want to ride the bus.
Bus too full.
I want to ride a bull.
Bull too black.
I want my money back.
Money too green.
I want a jellybean.
Bean too red.
I want to go to bed.
Bed too soft.
Throw the pillow off.
Close your eyes
And count to ten,
And if you mess up,
Start over again.

6

Silence in the court
While the judge blows his nose,
Stands on his head,
And tickles his toes.

Order in the court!
The judge is eating beans.
His wife is in the bathtub
Counting submarines.

The King of France
Lost his pants
Right in the middle
Of the wedding dance.

Ladies and gentlemen,
Take my advice,
Pull down your pants
And slide on the ice.

What's the time?
Half past nine.
Hang your knickers on the line.
When they're dry, bring 'em in.
Put 'em in the cookie tin.
Eat some cookies, eat some cake,
Eat your knickers by mistake.

COOKIES

Cinderella,
Dressed in yella,
Went downtown to meet her fella.
On the way
Her girdle busted.
How many people were disgusted?
1 - 2 - 3 - 4 - 5

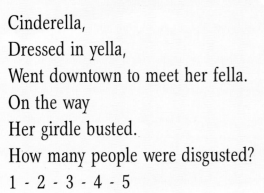

On the way Her girdle busted. How many people were disted? 1-2-3-4-5 Cinderella, Dressed in yella, Went downtown to meet her fella. On the wayr girdle busted. How m

9

Tarzan, Tarzan, through the air,
Tarzan lost his underwear.
Tarzan say, "Me don't care.
Jane buy me another pair."

Jane, Jane, through the air,
Jane lost her underwear.
Jane say, "Me don't care.
Boy buy me another pair."

Boy, Boy, through the air,
Boy lost his underwear.
Boy say, "Me don't care.
Cheetah buy me another pair."

Cheetah, Cheetah, through the air,
Cheetah lost his underwear.
Cheetah say, "Me don't care.
Monkeys don't need underwear."

11

Down, down, baby, down by the roller coaster.
Sweet, sweet baby, I'll never let you go.
Shimmy, shimmy, coca pop.
Shimmy, shimmy, pow!
Shimmy, shimmy, coca pop.
Shimmy, shimmy, pow!
Grandma, Grandma, sick in bed,
Called for the doctor and the doctor said,
"Let's get the rhythm of the head, *ding-dong!*
Let's get the rhythm of the head, *ding-dong!*
Let's get the rhythm of the hands, *clap, clap!*
Let's get the rhythm of the hands, *clap, clap!*
Let's get the rhythm of the feet, *stomp, stomp!*
Let's get the rhythm of the feet, *stomp, stomp!*"
Put it all together and what do you get?
Ding-dong, clap, clap, stomp, stomp.

Old man Moses, sick in bed,
Called for the doctor and the doctor said,
"Old man Moses, you're not sick.
All you need is a peppermint stick.
Clap your hands and turn around,
Do the boogaloo,
And get out of town."

13

Apple on a stick—
Make me sick,
Make my tummy go 2-4-6,
Not because I'm dirty,
Not because I'm clean,
Not because I kissed a boy behind a magazine.
Hcy, boys! How about a fight?
Here comes Johnny with his pants on tight!
He can wiggle, he can wobble, he can do the splits,
But I betcha twenty dollars that he can't do this!

(Followed by an amazing move by the rope skipper.)

14

BURP! Pardon me for being so rude.
It wasn't me, it was my food!
It didn't like it down below
And just popped up to say hello!

Nobody likes me, everybody hates me.
Guess I'll eat some worms.
Big fat juicy ones, long slim slimy ones,
Itsy bitsy fuzzy wuzzy worms.
First you bite their heads off,
Then you suck their guts out,
Then you throw the rest away.
Yum, yum!

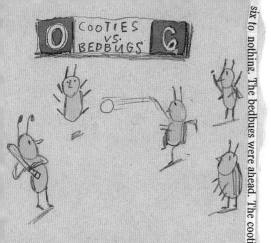

Oh, I won't go to Macy's any more, more, more.
There's a big fat policeman at the door, door, door.
He grabs me by the collar
And makes me pay a dollar,
So I won't go to Macy's any more, more, more.

I was standing in the corner,
Not doing any harm.
Along came a policeman
And took me by the arm.
He took me around the corner,
And he rang a little bell.
Along came a police car
And took me to my cell.
I woke up in the morning
And looked up on the wall.
The cooties and the bedbugs
Were having a game of ball.
The score was six to nothing.
The bedbugs were ahead.
The cooties hit a home run
And knocked me out of bed.

six to nothing. The bedbugs were ahead. The cooties hit a home run And knocked me out of bed. I was standing in the corner, Not doing any harm. Along came a policeman And took me by the arm.

16

Bubble gum, bubble gum, chew and blow,
Bubble gum, bubble gum, tap your toe,
Bubble gum, bubble gum, tastes so sweet,
Scrape that bubble gum off your feet!

Teacher, teacher, don't be dumb,
Give me back my bubble gum.
Teacher, teacher, don't be mean,
Give me a dollar for the soda machine.

Robin Hood and his Merry Men
Got to school at half past ten.
Teacher said, "You're late again,
Robin Hood and his Merry Men."

17

If you ever, ever, ever, ever, ever meet a bear,
You must never, never, never, never, never touch his hair,
'Cause if you ever, ever, ever, ever, ever touch his hair,
You will never, never, never, never meet another bear.

Teddy bear, teddy bear, turn around.
Teddy bear, teddy bear, touch the ground.
Teddy bear, teddy bear, show your shoe.
Teddy bear, teddy bear, I love you!
Teddy bear, teddy bear, go upstairs.
Teddy bear, teddy bear, say your prayers.
Teddy bear, teddy bear, turn off the light.
Teddy bear, teddy bear, say good night.

18

Hello, hello, hello, sir.
Meet me at the grocer.
No, sir.
Why, sir?
Because I have a cold, sir.
Where did you get the cold, sir?
At the North Pole, sir.
What were you doing there, sir?
Counting polar bears, sir.
How many did you count, sir?
1 - 2 - 3 - 4 - 5

Copycat, dirty rat,
Stole my mother's baseball bat.
Turned it in, turned it out,
Turned it into a speckled trout.

Liar, liar, pants on fire,
Nose as long as a telephone wire.

I'm rubber, you're glue.
Everything you say about me
Bounces off me and sticks to you.

20

Thank you for your portrait.
I think it's very nice.
I put it in the attic
To scare away the mice.

My mother, your mother live across the street.
They both live on Bubble Gum Street.
This is what they say when they get in a fight:
"Girls are dandy, made out of candy.
Boys are rotten, made out of cotton.
Girls go to Mars to get candy bars.
Boys go to Jupiter to get more stupider."

21

Roses are red,
Cabbages are green.
You've got a shape
Like a washing machine.

Roses are red,
Spiders are black.
Don't look now,
But there's one on your back!

Roses are red,
Licorice is black.
Do me a favor—
Go sit on a tack.

Roses are red,
Violets are blue.
Smelly socks
Remind me of you.

Roses are red,
Violets are blue.
Your nose is shaped
Like a B-52.

22

When Pinocchio was one, he learned to suck his thumb.
Thumb-ioka, thumb-ioka, half past one.
When Pinocchio was two, he learned to tie his shoe.
Shoe-ioka, shoe-ioka, half past two.
When Pinocchio was three, he learned to climb a tree.
Tree-ioka, tree-ioka, half past three.
When Pinocchio was four, he learned to shut the door.
Door-ioka, door-ioka, half past four.
When Pinocchio was five, he learned to skydive.
Dive-ioka, dive-ioka, half past five.
When Pinocchio was six, he learned to pick up sticks.
Stick-ioka, stick-ioka, half past six.
When Pinocchio was seven, he learned to go to heaven.
Heaven-ioka, heaven-ioka, half past seven.
When Pinocchio was eight, he learned to roller-skate.
Skate-ioka, skate-ioka, half past eight.
When Pinocchio was nine, he looked like Frankenstein.
Stein-ioka, stein-ioka, half past nine.
When Pinocchio was ten, he married a big red hen.
Hen-ioka, hen-ioka, half past ten.

I love myself, I think I'm grand.
I go to the movies. I hold my hand.
I put my arm around my waist.
When I get fresh, I slap my face.

Ladies and jellybeans, hoboes and tramps,
Cross-eyed mosquitoes and bow-legged ants,
I come before you to stand behind you
To tell you something I know nothing about.
Next Monday, which is Good Friday,
There will be a mothers' meeting for fathers only.
Admission is free, so pay at the door.
Pull up a chair and sit on the floor.
It doesn't really matter where you sit,
'Cause the boy on the balcony's sure to spit.

I went to the movies tomorrow
And took a front seat at the back.
I fell from the floor to the ceiling
And hurt the front part of my back.

Coca-Cola went to town,
Diet Pepsi knocked him down.
Dr Pepper fixed him up.
Now I'm drinking Seven-Up.
Seven-Up caught the flu,
Now I'm drinking Mountain Dew.
Mountain Dew fell off the mountain,
Now I'm drinking from the water fountain.

Not last night, but the night before,
A lemon and a pickle came knocking at my door.
I went downstairs to let them in.
They hit me on the head with a rolling pin.

Miss Sue, Miss Sue,
Miss Sue from Alabama—
Her real name's Susianna.
Sittin' in a rockin' chair,
Eatin' Betty Crocker,
Watchin' the clock go
Tick-tock, tick-tock,
Banana rock.
A-B-C-D-E-F-G,
Wash the spots right offa me.
Booshka, booshka,
Freeze!

Mrs. Brown
Went to town
With her knickers hanging down.
She had a nickel.
She bought a pickle.
The pickle was sour.
She picked a flower.
The flower was yellow.
She bought her a fellow.
The fellow was mean.
She bought a bean.
The bean was hard.
She bought a card.
And on the card
It said, "Red-hot pepper!"

Did you ever, ever, ever in your bow-legged life
Meet a bow-legged sailor and his bow-legged wife?
No, I never, never, never in my bow-legged life
Met a bow-legged sailor and his bow-legged wife.

Did you ever, ever, ever in your knock-kneed life
Meet a knock-kneed sailor and his knock-kneed wife?
No, I never, never, never in my knock-kneed life
Met a knock-kneed sailor and his knock-kneed wife.

Did you ever, ever, ever in your spoon-headed life
Meet a spoon-headed sailor and his spoon-headed wife?
No, I never, never, never in my spoon-headed life
Met a spoon-headed sailor and his spoon-headed wife.

I am a pretty little Dutch girl,
As pretty as can be, be, be,
And all the guys on the football team
Are crazy over me, me, me.
I have a boyfriend, Tony.
He's made of macaroni,
With forty-four toes and a big fat nose.
And this is how my story goes:
One day when I was walking,
I saw my boyfriend talking
To a pretty little girl with a strawberry curl,
And this is what he said to her:
"I L-O-V-E love you,
I K-I-S-S kiss you,"
So he jumped in a lake
And swallowed a snake
And came out with a bellyache.

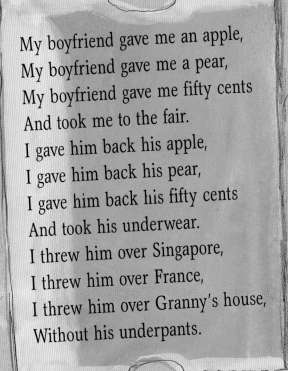

My boyfriend gave me an apple,
My boyfriend gave me a pear,
My boyfriend gave me fifty cents
And took me to the fair.
I gave him back his apple,
I gave him back his pear,
I gave him back his fifty cents
And took his underwear.
I threw him over Singapore,
I threw him over France,
I threw him over Granny's house,
Without his underpants.

My mother gave me a nickel.
My father gave me a dime.
My sister gave me a boyfriend
Who kissed me all the time.
My mother took my nickel.
My father took my dime.
My sister took my boyfriend
And gave me Frankenstein.
He made me wash the dishes,
He made me mop the floor.
I didn't like his attitude,
So I kicked him out the door!

For Maxine
—J.S.

For Samantha
—M.S.

THIS IS A BORZOI BOOK PUBLISHED BY ALFRED A. KNOPF
Text copyright © 2005 by Judy Sierra. Illustrations copyright © 2005 by Melissa Sweet.
All rights reserved under International and Pan-American Copyright Conventions. Published in the
United States by Alfred A. Knopf, an imprint of Random House Children's Books, a division of
Random House, Inc., New York, and simultaneously in Canada by Random House of Canada Limited,
Toronto. Distributed by Random House, Inc., New York.
KNOPF, BORZOI BOOKS, and the colophon are registered trademarks of Random House, Inc.
www.randomhouse.com/kids

Library of Congress Cataloging-in-Publication Data
Sierra, Judy.
Schoolyard rhymes / by Judy Sierra ; illustrated by Melissa Sweet. — 1st ed.
p.   cm.
ISBN 0-375-82516-9 (trade) — ISBN 0-375-92516-3 (lib. bdg.)
1. Games—Juvenile literature. 2. Rhyming games—Juvenile literature.
3. Singing games—Juvenile literature. I. Sweet, Melissa, ill. II. Title.
GV1203.S525 2005
398.8—dc22
2004004273

MANUFACTURED IN CHINA
July 2005
10 9 8 7 6 5 4 3 2 1
First Edition

Index of First Lines